NIGHT
IS A
ROOM

NIGHT
IS A
ROOM

NAOMI
WALLACE

THEATRE COMMUNICATIONS GROUP / NEW YORK / 2016

Night Is a Room is published by Theatre Communications Group, Inc.,
520 Eighth Avenue, 24th Floor, New York, NY 10018-4156

Epigraphs: "One-Way Street" by Walter Benjamin, *One-Way Street and Other Writings*, published by NLB, London, 1979. "Complaint" by William Carlos Williams, *The Collected Poems of William Carlos Williams*, published by New Directions, New York, 1986. "Jerusalem" by William Blake, *Jerusalem*, published by The William Blake Trust/Princeton University Press, Princeton, New Jersey, 1998.

The publication of *Night Is a Room* by Naomi Wallace, through TCG's Book Program, is made possible in part by the New York State Council on the Arts with the support of Governor Andrew Cuomo and the New York State Legislature.

TCG books are exclusively distributed to the book trade by Consortium Book Sales and Distribution.

Library of Congress Control Numbers:
2016039314 (print) / 2016045562 (ebook)
ISBN 978-1-55936-518-5 (paperback) / ISBN 978-1-55936-844-5 (ebook)
A catalog record for this book is available from the Library of Congress.

Cover design, book design and composition by Lisa Govan
Cover art by Bruce McLeod

First Edition, December 2016

The only way of knowing a person is to love them without hope.

—WALTER BENJAMIN, "ONE-WAY STREET"

Night is a room
darkened for lovers

—WILLIAM CARLOS WILLIAMS, "COMPLAINT"

I drew forth the pang
Of sorrow red hot:
I work'd it on my resolute anvil.

—WILLIAM BLAKE, "JERUSALEM"

Night Is a Room had its world premiere at Signature Theatre (James Houghton, Artistic Director; Erika Mallin, Executive Director) in New York, on November 22, 2015. It was directed by Bill Rauch. The scenic design was by Rachel Hauck, the costume design was by Clint Ramos, the lighting design was by Jen Schriever and the sound design was by Leah Gelpe. The production stage manager was Cole P. Bonenberger. The cast was:

LIANA	Dagmara Dominczyk
MARCUS	Bill Heck
DORÉ	Ann Dowd

Characters may flow from one idea or subject to the next, even if there seems to be no obvious connection between lines. As though the link between thoughts is sometimes missing, but perhaps only for us. Some lines have no break between them and should be treated as complete sentences. Accents are light, not "realistic." Liana and Marcus have a mild standard English accent. Doré has a light Yorkshire accent.

A beat is one second long. A period within a line signals a break, a half second. When compelled, ignore either or both. A forward slash signals an interruption at the end of the word.

ACT ONE

Lights up on Doré and Liana. They are standing in the back garden of a small working-class ground-floor flat. A couple of simple vintage 1970s indoor chairs have been brought outside as lawn chairs. The grass is sparse. There is a small pile of stones for a project abandoned. There is a tray for tea set on a chair. The tea has not yet been poured. Liana is elegantly but subtly dressed, having just come from her office. She has a courier bag with her. Doré has put on her better clothes for the occasion, which also have a 1970s feel. Doré is shy and subdued, which almost hides her quick intelligence. She will rarely look directly at Liana during the scene, and unless indicated, Doré will gaze intently elsewhere, though her gaze is neither vacant nor passive.

LIANA: I've brought balloons. We've a choice of colors.

(Liana begins to take small bags of balloons out of her courier bag. Doré watches with fascination.)

Red? Green? Blue? You must have a favorite color. How about orange?

(Doré just looks on, still stunned by Liana's presence.)

Ah, these are fancy! One color inside another. A two-layer balloon. Red inside yellow. Blue inside green. And even a few with tiny bells inside so when you blow them up and flick them, you hear bells. *(Beat)* Shall I blow one up?

(Doré nods. Liana blows up a balloon, first stretching it to loosen it up. It gets bigger. And bigger. Liana examines it. Decides it needs to be a bit bigger and blows some more. Then she ties it off.)

For you.

(Liana hands it to Doré, who takes it hesitantly, almost as though it were alive. She gazes inside it at the tiny bell.)

See the tiny bell inside?

(Doré nods.)

Shake it.

(Doré looks doubtful.)

It won't bite. Go on.

(Doré shakes the balloon weakly. The tiny bell sounds. Doré smiles for the first time. Liana laughs. Doré shakes it harder; the bell sounds louder.)

Such a cheerful sound!

(Doré shakes it again. Harder. The balloon pops. Both women freeze.)

Never mind. I've lots more.

(Doré, with her eyes, searches for the bell that fell out of the balloon. She can't see it. Then she meets Liana's eyes briefly. It's awkward.)

We'll have some tea then?

(Liana fills the cups, though Doré doesn't touch hers.)

You're not an easy woman to find. It took me quite a few weeks of searching. Intense searching, to find you. And a pretty penny.

DORÉ: You paid to find me?

LIANA: I certainly couldn't do it on my own.

DORÉ: How much?

LIANA: Well.

DORÉ: To find me?

LIANA: It's just money.

(Doré waits to hear the amount. Intent.)

Two thousand pounds.

(Doré gasps.)

Yes. Two thousand.

DORÉ: I wasn't hiding.

LIANA: Of course not.

DORÉ: I didn't know you were looking.

LIANA: It's worth every penny.

(Liana relaxes.)

I'd like to know something about you. Doré. You don't mind. *(Beat)* Whatever you choose to tell me.

(Doré is quiet.)

Anything. I'm sure there's nothing you can tell me that I won't find fascinating.

(Liana waits. After a moment Doré speaks. She does not rush her words. Her words flow without typical breaks. At other times her speech is more conventional.)

DORÉ: When I go to the market on the weekends I wear my slippers no one notices they almost look like outdoor shoes and much warmer.

LIANA: Oh. I see.

DORÉ: I'm wearing them now.

LIANA *(Looking at Doré's feet)*: They look toasty. I wouldn't have guessed—

DORÉ: These have lasted seventeen years.

LIANA: —if I saw your feet in the market. Saw you at the market.

(Doré is uncertain again. Liana notices the chairs.)

These are beautiful. Vintage 1970s, I believe?

DORÉ: My house is full of the stuff it was new back then modern made to last my father bought the furniture for me in Paris and had it shipped.

LIANA: Your father has good taste.

DORÉ: Yes he did.

(Another silence. But Liana pushes on.)

LIANA: So. What do you enjoy? In your spare time?

DORÉ: I like to do Sudoku at the back of the newspaper those little squares all waiting for me imagine someone thinks it up everyday maybe a computer I don't know but there they are for me I've always been good at numbers I skip the news it's gossip mostly grubby isn't it?

(Liana is not really listening but rather eyeing up the surroundings, though it seems she might be also replying to Doré.)

LIANA *(Almost to herself)*: Depressing.
DORÉ: I don't like paying for it.
LIANA: Gloomy.
DORÉ: TV is worse.
LIANA: Almost sinister, definitely ominous.
DORÉ: Never any good news.
LIANA: One would be hard-pressed to make anything of it.
DORÉ: Right. So I turn straight to the back seems a waste of paper I've been thinking of buying one of those books but I'd almost feel guilty like I was indulging myself.
LIANA *(To herself)*: Though I could get decorators in—

(Doré claps her hands together, and this catches Liana's attention.)

DORÉ: The lottery numbers each week I like to add them up then divide them by the day of the week as fast as I can and then times them by the month I can look at a number any long number and break it down quicker than you can crack an egg do you like eggs?
LIANA: Oh. Yes. I like them scrambled.
DORÉ: I don't like eggs but I like the sound when they break do you?
LIANA: I'm not sure. Let me think. *(Beat)* I do seem to remember a satisfying crack.
DORÉ: Yes. A good "crack."

LIANA: I assume you've. Worked all these years?

DORÉ: Still do.

(Silence between them. Liana waits.)

LIANA: Ah. Then please tell me what jobs you've held. Hold.

DORÉ: Well really I don't hold them the jobs hold me or rather they grip me around the neck and begin to squeeze so slow you think it's sleep coming on but it's suffocation.

LIANA: I'm sorry.

DORÉ: I've a thick neck and good lungs and suffocation you know does have its rewards.

LIANA: It does. It does?

(Doré glances for the lost bell again.)

Your life's been hard.

DORÉ: My life?

LIANA: Perhaps we could be of help.

DORÉ: We.

LIANA: I mean myself and /

DORÉ: Please. Blow up another balloon?

(Liana blows up another balloon.)

It looks so tiny in all that space. Why only one bell?

(Liana shrugs. Doré shakes the balloon and the bell sounds.)

DORÉ: It's cruel.

LIANA: It's a balloon.

DORÉ: It's a bell a bell in a balloon imagine if we were inside there a giant balloon tiny me tiny you and someone gave us a good shake what sound would we make?

LIANA: Perhaps not like bells.

DORÉ: Perhaps not what a shame I work in other people's homes perhaps I worked in your home once.

LIANA: No. I'd remember you.

DORÉ: You think so?

LIANA: I'm certain.

DORÉ: It's hard to remember our faces because we're mostly turned to the floor do you clean?

LIANA: Oh. In between.

DORÉ: In between.

LIANA: In between the day our. Cleaner comes to our home.

DORÉ: What does she look like?

LIANA: She's twenty-nine. She's tall! From Poland. She snorts when she laughs.

DORÉ: Snorts when she laughs?

LIANA: Yes. It's a funny little sound.

DORÉ: Show me please.

LIANA: I. I don't know how to snort.

DORÉ: Of course you do.

LIANA: Well. I could try.

DORÉ: Please try.

(Liana tries to snort, but she's restrained.)

That's not really a snort.

LIANA: It's hard to replicate. It's quite original, the sound our Kasia makes.

DORÉ: Our Kasia.

LIANA: Yes, I mean myself and my /

DORÉ: Let me give it a try.

(Doré makes herself laugh. She begins small, then gets more involved in it. She laughs and laughs, then begins to snort as she laughs. It's a good snort. Then she is suddenly silent.)

What color are Kasia's eyes?

(Liana doesn't know the answer. She looks at her watch.)

LIANA: We were talking about you.

(Liana waits, then lets it go.)

Well, as for myself, I'm a senior account director.

DORÉ *(Impressed)*: Oh. *(Beat)* What's that?

LIANA: It's the senior point of contact for an ad agency's customers, the liaison between clients and the agency. I manage pitches, make sure the account is running profitably. Usually I handle four to five noncompeting accounts at a time. I make sure everyone and everything is working in unison, that the same message is getting across in all mediums. *(Laughs)* I'm a bit like the conductor of an orchestra really, only without the harp or violins. Though now and then I /

DORÉ: There's the bell. Watch out!

(Doré lunges for the tiny bell. Liana is startled and takes a wrong step, twisting the heel off her shoe.)

LIANA: Ow. Damn it.

(She examines her shoe.)

The heel's come off.

DORÉ *(Disappointed)*: Oh. It's not the bell. Just a bit of glass. These stupid old stones.

(Doré gives the stones a swift kick, as though they were a bad dog.)

I've been meaning to build a garden wall I should just have them cleared away are you all right?

(Liana puts her shoe back on again. Now she walks with a slight limp.)

LIANA: I don't much like these shoes anyway.
DORÉ: That's lucky then.

(Doré gazes at the broken heel.)

I hope you can get it fixed?
LIANA: Leave it. It's not worth the trouble.
DORÉ: I recommend slippers there's no heel to lose.

(For the first time Liana holds Doré's gaze.)

LIANA: He'll be forty on Friday.
DORÉ *(Quickly, simply)*: I know.
LIANA: Of course you do. Now, Marcus works only a half day on Friday. I was thinking that we could /
DORÉ: Is that his name?

(For the first time Doré sits down.)

Marcus.
LIANA: Marcus, yes.
DORÉ: Jonathan. *(Beat)* I always thought of him as Jonathan.
LIANA: Well, you'll want to know a bit about Marcus, of course. Before. About us.

(Doré gazes into her hands.)

Well. Let's see then. *(Beat)* He's handsome! Oh yes he is. The first time I saw Marcus was in Roundhay Park. He was leaning with his back against a tree.

(At the mention of the tree, Doré startles.)

DORÉ: A tree?

LIANA: Yes. A tall tree with a gigantic trunk. His eyes were closed. My first thought was, "He's ill." My second thought was, "Perhaps he's mad." He looked so. Peaceful. As though the trunk were holding him up. As though he were a part of it. I watched him for a while. I don't know for how long. His quiet made me feel quiet, too. Then he suddenly opened his eyes and looked straight into mine. I had to catch my breath for it felt as though he'd reached down inside me and squeezed the air from my lungs. Then we both laughed. Two strangers laughing together before we even spoke. It all seemed so /

DORÉ: What kind of tree was it?

LIANA: What?

DORÉ: That he was leaning against. What kind of tree?

LIANA: I don't know.

DORÉ: It must have been a maple.

LIANA: It could have been. Any tree, I suppose.

DORÉ: A maple what color are his eyes?

LIANA: Green. Dark green. We've been married for twenty-one years.

(Doré picks up the broken heel and holds it out to Liana.)

DORÉ: You should take this just in case I'm sorry.

LIANA: Please, just throw it away. No worries.

(At some point as they speak, Doré will, almost unconsciously, put the broken heel in her pocket.)

Marcus is assistant head of Skipton Girls' High School. A bit of a commute for him from Leeds, but he relishes the work, says it keeps him young. The girls adore him. Some of them have taken to calling him The Knight because he once arrived for his nine A.M. on the Middle Ages dressed in full armor. He knows how to spark even the most taciturn of students.

(*Doré doesn't respond. Silence between them.*)

Marcus's adoptive parents are now both dead. They were an older couple when they adopted.

DORÉ: He misses them?

LIANA: They were very good to him.

DORÉ: I don't know if I can.

LIANA: Of course you can.

DORÉ (*Shaking her head*): So many years.

LIANA: It's just time.

(*Doré looks straight at Liana, wondering.*)

DORÉ: He doesn't suspect anything?

LIANA: Has no idea. It will be his birthday gift. (*Beat*) Actually, I've thought about doing this for years but I always had a hunch that his fortieth would be just the right year. For the two of you. To meet.

DORÉ: He won't agree.

LIANA: I'll say it's a surprise. I'll tell him that he must come to this address at four P.M. on Friday. And not to be a minute late. He'll do it. He'll think it's just a surprise party of friends from work. And then you and I will be here to welcome him. I can't wait to see his face. I expect he'll jump out of his shoes.

DORÉ: He'll be upset.

LIANA: But that will only be the first stage and it will pass. I have a colleague at work, Emma, who met her biological father for the first time when she was forty-five. It was a shock, even though she set it up. But she said that in the end it was a gift, that her tiny, frightened, child-within was able to /

DORÉ: She was pregnant at the time?

LIANA: What? No, Emma was— Oh! No, no, I mean "child-within" as a way of speaking about the experiences we've had as children, that we carry those same experiences inside us, as one would a child.

DORÉ: Carrying a child is not the same as carrying an experience.

LIANA: Of course not. But what I mean to say is that Emma said that after meeting her father, she was finally able to grow up and embrace the world. That she felt . . . freed and able to live life more fully. *(Beat)* I want to give that to my husband. I love him very much.

(Doré thinks some moments. She nods. It seems she's going to say "yes.")

DORÉ: No.

LIANA: Please don't say that.

DORÉ: It's not a good idea.

LIANA: But it is. It will be, for both of you, after the initial . . . There will be tears, yes. Emotional turbulence, anger even, followed by various stages of grief and loss, but then the release. Catharsis. Shocking but deeply satisfying, painful but terribly necessary. But most of all, joy. Joy for Marcus. And joy for you.

(Liana uses her last card.)

And then perhaps one day soon. You can meet. Your granddaughter.

(Doré makes a small sound, as though to catch her breath.)

Her name is Dominique.

(Doré turns her head away, as though burned. Liana continues carefully.)

We call her Dom. She's just finished university, at Warwick, and now she's in Chicago, at the Art Institute. Though she lives in a frightening place called Little Village. On . . . South Marshall Boulevard.

(Doré moves away from Liana, to get some air.)

I've told her to get a better flat, that we'll help with the rent. You can't be too safe in Chicago. But she's an independent one, Dom is. She loves it there, says she's never been so cold in her life. *(Beat)* It's perfectly normal that you're apprehensive. But I promise you. Doré.

(At the sound of her name, Doré looks at Liana.)

After all these years, to finally confront, to acknowledge and embrace /

(Doré looks away and her eyes fall on the lost bell.)

DORÉ: There's the bell!

(She picks it up.)

Oh. It's been stepped on flattened.

(Doré tries to make the bell ring but it's silent.)

LIANA: It's just junk.

(Doré tries again.)

DORÉ: It made a lovely sound. *(Beat)* Is my. Son. Has he . . . ?

(Doré falters.)

LIANA: Ask me anything.

DORÉ: Has he been faithful to you?

LIANA: Christ. *(Laughs)* What a question. Something so. Intimate. It's rude, really.

(Doré just waits.)

Yes. He has.

DORÉ *(Fact)*: You're lying.

LIANA: Of course I'm lying. It's none of my business. Your business.

DORÉ: I'm sorry.

LIANA: In the beginning there were a few slips.

DORÉ: Slips.

LIANA: That's what we call them. Marcus and I. We were walking along together in our marriage, side by side, and we slipped.

DORÉ: Both of you at the same time? Why was it so icy?

LIANA: We weren't taking the time to be friends, to confide in one another. But there have been no more slips since our early years. Marriages are imploding all around us but we're still together. Faithfully and happily. We count ourselves extremely lucky.

DORÉ: Did you have a slip?

LIANA: Once.

DORÉ: For how long?

LIANA: Not long. And I confessed.

DORÉ: Was he upset?

LIANA: He wept like a child for weeks. I have to say I had little patience for it. He'd had a handful of slips and I never wallowed. I'd shout, have a good cry, break something. Then I'd have a shower and be done with it. You see,

I've never doubted Marcus's love for me. I think he just needed to disappear on occasion.

DORÉ: Slip.

LIANA: Yes, until he found his footing. We all make mistakes.

DORÉ: Yes we do. You're very beautiful.

LIANA: Thank you. Do you have someone special?

DORÉ: Oh no. No . . .

LIANA: You never married?

DORÉ: For a few years but I don't remember them he was bald I remember that I don't recall his voice or anything he ever said to me where do they go all those words filling the air filling a room so many of them 'til there's no more space for either of you any longer you get crowded out. *(Beat)* I'll do it. For his birthday.

LIANA: Yes! Thank you, Doré. Thank you.

DORÉ: But on one condition.

LIANA: Anything.

DORÉ: I'd like for you not to be here.

LIANA: Oh.

DORÉ: Just not this very first time you understand.

LIANA: I could wait outside, then. Or upstairs. You could call me when you're /

DORÉ: Just him. No one else.

LIANA: Well.

DORÉ: It's not personal you understand.

LIANA: I think I do. Yes. This first meeting will naturally be. Unexpected. Perhaps even a shock. A real challenge for the both of you. *(Beat)* All right. As you wish. And I should be going. Four P.M. then? Friday.

DORÉ: Yes.

LIANA: Even if at first it's distressing, what follows will be a celebration. Try and enjoy the occasion. I'll have ginger cake sent over as well. He loves ginger.

(Liana gathers up her things to leave.)

So I'll leave the balloons. There's enough here. Will you have a problem inflating them?

(Doré shakes her head.)

Excellent. *(Beat)* One day you'll thank me for. Arranging this reunion.

DORÉ *(Looks up at Liana)*: Orchestrating?

LIANA: Exactly. *(Beat)* You don't have to be without your son any longer.

(Doré is quiet. Liana nods, confident, and begins to leave.)

DORÉ: Liana.

(The women meet each other's eyes. Liana is pleased to hear her name used.)

LIANA: Yes, Doré?

DORÉ: I've never been without my son.

ACT TWO

Three weeks later. Sunday afternoon.

The living room space of Marcus and Liana's home. The residence is upper middle class. The room is sparse. The few pieces of furniture are mostly covered; redecorating is making its slow progress. A low coffee table and three nice chairs have been partly uncovered for the occasion, for afternoon tea and cake. Marcus is dressed comfortably but still smart. He has Liana pinned in a chair. They are both laughing and struggling with each other.

LIANA: No. No! Quit. Quit it.

MARCUS: We've got twenty minutes.

LIANA: That's not enough time!

MARCUS: But we skipped our last few dates.

LIANA: Redecorating always slows us down.

(They struggle.)

MARCUS: Do you really want to stop me?

(Marcus manages to thrust his hand into Liana's trousers. She resists again, but not enough to dislodge him. He touches her. She grips his arm to try and stop him, but then, after some moments, she is helping him.)

Know what I love about you? Steven. Who teaches chemistry? He says it takes his wife four full minutes to get really wet. He's timed it. But you . . .

LIANA: Shut up . . .

(Liana begins to make small sounds of pleasure. Marcus is behind the chair now, leaning over her.)

MARCUS: Extraordinary. With one finger I can turn on the taps.

(Liana slaps his face, quite hard.)

LIANA: You bragging bastard.
MARCUS: A grateful, bragging bastard. You're gorgeous.
LIANA *(Breathless)*: Let me touch you.
MARCUS: Not now.
LIANA: But I want to touch you.

(Liana reaches to touch him but he won't let her touch him.)

MARCUS: Just for you this time. You're so very beautiful, darling . . .

(Marcus's fingers move deeper inside her.)

LIANA: My God you're romantic today . . . Did you get a raise? . . . A bonus?
MARCUS: You're a celestial sphere inside . . .
LIANA: Ah . . . Teaching the Renaissance again . . . Always gets you spunky . . .

(Liana gets closer to cumming.)

MARCUS: Louder. I want to hear you.

(The phone rings, loudly, just as Liana cums. On the fourth ring Liana picks it up, composing herself quickly.)

LIANA: Hello? *(Beat)* Oh, hello darling . . . No. Not at all. We were just. Redecorating. *(Beat)* Everything all right? *(Beat)* Oh. The bank said it went out Thursday. *(Beat)* Well it's not like it used to be. All those security checks on transfers slow things down. Wires can take up to three days now, at least.

(As Liana talks, Marcus takes a napkin from the table and, with relish, carefully dries his hand, his fingers, as he watches Liana, who shoes him away. Liana arranges herself as she speaks. Marcus hands her the napkin and she quickly wipes herself.)

Yes. I got that one yesterday. No. I didn't get the nude. Send it again. You might have to compress the file.

(Liana throws the used napkin playfully at Marcus.)

I do love the charcoal drawing of those woods. They look so. Black and dead. *(Beat)* I didn't mean that in a negative way. Of course there's life to it! I just mean dead things can be so . . . lively, don't you think? *(Beat)* Exactly. *(Beat)* All right. We'll call you in a few. Be safe. Act like you know the streets.

MARCUS: Tell Dom I love her. Very much.

(Marcus looks to throw the napkin in the bin but there's no bin in sight, so he pockets it.)

LIANA: Your father says he loves you very much.

MARCUS *(A bit too seriously)*: He says: the verys never end.

LIANA: He says, "The verys never end." *(Beat)* Yes, you too. Love you. Bye.

(Liana hangs up. Silence a moment.)

Dom's truly happy there. So far from us and so happy.

MARCUS: She can forget all about us. That's how secure she is. We did a good job, didn't we?

LIANA: I miss her.

MARCUS: So do I. Sometimes my chest literally aches for her.

(Liana just looks at Marcus. For a moment she's concerned.)

LIANA: Are you all right? Something like that could be medical.

MARCUS: No, it's just a. I'm fine.

(Liana nods.)

The head at school has suggested I apply for deputy.

LIANA: But Marcus, that's wonder /

MARCUS: Yes. But it means more admin, and less teaching.

LIANA: But also a raise. Congratulations. You deserve it.

MARCUS: But it's the teaching that keeps me going: all those small, eager faces—

LIANA: You're very good.

MARCUS: —imploring me, begging me to feed them the facts, to give them the answers, no questions asked, just the answers; it doesn't matter to them if they can use what I give them because they don't want to think or take a position: *Please sir, just give us the facts.* So I tell these young ladies that statistically one in ten of them, or something like that, will die over the coming holidays; which one of you will it be, I ask? How's that for a fact?

LIANA: That's cruel, darling.

MARCUS: I want to see their faces crumple with doubt, with misgiving, disbelief, outrage; I want them to feel something other than recording the facts about medicine through time or the Holocaust, the American West, Hiroshima; to get behind the notes, to sense on their skin that the facts are as alive as they are. But it's like a quagmire and each day I wade in to retrieve the fucking actualities, dead and rotten and floating on the surface.

LIANA: Marcus?

MARCUS: Why shouldn't we throw out the certainties, surprise ourselves and all the little expectant faces sucking at the tit of fact, at the factory— I just thought of that—the factory; free up history . . .

LIANA: And?

MARCUS: I don't know. Free up history and . . .

LIANA: Isn't that a little dangerous, darling? History as bunk?

MARCUS: No. I mean. Yes, maybe it is but sometimes I feel like a tour guide wandering through a graveyard pointing out this or that historical fact. I want them to feel the past on their skin. I want to feel it.

(Silence a moment. Liana wonders at Marcus's outburst, but then she looks at her watch.)

LIANA: I hope your mother isn't having trouble finding the address.

MARCUS: I drew her a map.

LIANA: How strange.

MARCUS: What is?

LIANA: That I'm saying, "I hope your mother isn't having trouble finding the address." We've never said something like that before, between the two of us. And now it just slips out of my mouth like it's always been there.

MARCUS: You think she'll like the house?

LIANA: Well you've seen hers, of course she'll like it.

MARCUS: Maybe we should sit in the garden.

LIANA: This is fine, darling. She'll be impressed with how well you've done. It's about time she comes here. I'm flexible but I won't have you away visiting every evening.

MARCUS: It's not been every evening. And just these last three weeks.

LIANA: No, but you're home at eleven and ten is our bedtime. From now on, please bring her here more often. Then we can all have a visit and I will see more of my husband.

MARCUS: She's very reserved. Very shy.

LIANA: She is. I had to give her a good squeeze to get her to tell me anything about herself. And even then there wasn't much /

MARCUS: She's very smart, you know.

LIANA: Is she? Oh. I hadn't— Okay.

MARCUS: She's never had a proper education but she reads an enormous amount.

LIANA: Does she?

MARCUS: And quite widely too. Not the good stuff, but with a little careful guidance she could be persuaded. And she does watercolors on the weekends. Birds. Trees. You can definitely see there's a bit of talent there. She's very precise. And she showed me a couple of rare, old art books from the '20s she found at a boot sale. She'd like to give them to Dominique.

LIANA: I'm sure Dom has all the art books she needs.

MARCUS: Of course. But it's a kind thought.

LIANA: Yes it is.

(A silence in which Liana feels comfortable.)

She's a solitary woman. Even when I stood close to her it seemed she was alone.

(Marcus is quiet.)

I'd bet she thought her life would never change. That it would keep to the same track. Then I walked through her door. And now you'll be at her bedside.

MARCUS *(Startled)*: What do you mean?

LIANA: You'll be at her bedside when she dies.

MARCUS: Oh, yes. Of course.

LIANA: It must be an unimaginable comfort for her to wake up in the morning and suddenly she's got you!

(Liana looks her husband over admiringly.)

And what a striking man you are. And tonight we'll go to bed early so we can have a good read in bed. But before we do that, I'll lay you down on this floor and open your trouser buttons one by one, with my teeth. Then I'm going to suck your cock. I won't tire; my tongue never does. I'll tease you until you're furious and rigid in my mouth. When you finally cum I want you to cum so hard—

MARCUS: —that I knock out the back of your throat—

LIANA: —and scramble my brains!

(They both laugh, a little breathless, a little silly. Then Marcus stops smiling and is serious.)

MARCUS: In all these years.

LIANA *(Unsure but still playful)*: What? *(Beat)* What is it?

MARCUS: I want you to. I know that I. *(Beat)* Liana—

(Before Marcus can finish, Doré appears. She is still shy, though perhaps a little less so. She is initially uncomfortable in unfamiliar surroundings, and still rarely looks either Marcus or Liana directly in the face.)

DORÉ: I knocked a few times. Hello!

LIANA: Doré! I'm so glad you're here. We were just babbling and didn't hear you knock.

DORÉ: I didn't want to use the bell.

(She greets Marcus, but with reserve, hardly glancing at him.)

Hello.

LIANA: Come here. Let me hug you.

(Liana hugs her. Doré is stiff but then begins to respond just as Liana pulls away.)

Now please sit down. You'll have some tea. And do forgive how bare it is in here. We're redecorating and most of the furniture's in storage.

DORÉ: That's nice.

LIANA: Just the usual. A new color on the wall, new curtains. Every six years we do it. We enjoy the change.

DORÉ: The walls are a lovely yellow.

LIANA: Well, it will be a pale orange as soon as our painter remembers us.

MARCUS: And the plastering.

LIANA: He's always five or six months behind. Isn't he, Marcus?

MARCUS: He does an excellent job once he starts. I think he missed being born during the fifteenth century. He seems to think plastering a wall is preparing for a fresco and insists that the plaster has a life of its own, adventurously reacting to the light, air and various pressures of his brushes. On top of it, he believes he's reinventing color. The bastard looks down his nose at us when we insist on paying him!

(The women laugh.)

LIANA: How are you?

DORÉ *(Earnestly)*: I'm well, Liana.

LIANA: I can imagine.

DORÉ: Can you?

LIANA: Of course, darling. I do have an imagination. That's our secret: we self-described Advert Whores.

DORÉ: Oh my.

LIANA: Oh yes. Though often seen as money-grubbing executives of mass deception, intent on finding the precise instrument to stir the soul into spending its last pound of silver, we're more like poets, really. We find the "it" and then find a way to say it in other words. Our best jingles are set in iambic pentameter, metaphor as bribe and promise, image as loophole, as exemption from the rest /

DORÉ: I had no idea.

LIANA: So in these weeks I've deployed this same imagination dozens of times to picture how it would be if I hadn't seen Dom since she was born. I shudder when I imagine it but I try and understand. The joy. I think I'd explode with it.

(Doré thinks for some moments.)

DORÉ: It's not really an explosion is it Jonathan?

MARCUS: No, I suppose it's not.

DORÉ: It's more like a bang but without the sound.

LIANA: Jonathan?

DORÉ: Oh. I'm sorry. *(To Marcus)* You didn't tell her I call you Jonathan? *(To Liana)* It just felt too foreign to call him by his other name.

LIANA: But Marcus is not his other name. Marcus is his legal name.

DORÉ: Yes but Jonathan just comes out naturally I hope you don't mind too very much?

LIANA: Well . . .

MARCUS (*To Doré*): Would you like a piece of cake? It's orange cake.

DORÉ: Yes please anything orange delights me.

(*Marcus gets her cake. Liana just watches. Marcus spills the cake into Doré's lap.*)

Oopsie.

MARCUS: I'm so sorry. What a klutz . . .

DORÉ: No harm done.

(*Gingerly, he picks a few of the larger cake bits from Doré's lap.*)

LIANA: I'll do it, Marcus. Why don't you get a cloth from the kitchen?

(*Marcus steps into the kitchen. Liana bends over Doré and deftly sweeps the cake from Doré's lap onto a saucer. Suddenly Doré can't resist and she clasps Liana's face in her two hands. She kisses her hard on the forehead.*)

DORÉ: You were right Liana thank you thank you.

(*Liana smiles. Both women share an intense moment. When Marcus reappears he sees their intimacy and just stops and stares until Liana sees him and pulls away. Doré quickly wipes a tear away.*)

I'll take that.

(Marcus hands Doré the cloth and she tidies herself up. She tastes a piece of the broken cake.)

Delicious. Did you make it?

LIANA: Yes. I like to bake.

DORÉ *(Sincerely)*: But how does a senior account director find time?

MARCUS: She bakes even when she doesn't have the time.

LIANA: Please. Let's all sit.

(Marcus remains standing.)

DORÉ: I won't stay long. I know how busy /

LIANA: Nonsense. The afternoon is yours.

DORÉ: How kind of you to say so.

(There is an awkward silence for some moments. Doré makes a few furtive glances at Marcus.)

What should we talk about then?

LIANA: Well. There are so many things.

(Silence. We hear the sound of spoons in cups.)

DORÉ: I'll start I'll tell her about the tree yes Jonathan?

MARCUS: The tree?

DORÉ: My dreams, you silly.

MARCUS: Oh. Why don't we talk about. My teaching. I was thinking that this term I would do something different for art history and dress up as Cellini's Perseus. I've already got the shorts and the sword—though Medusa's head might be a challenge /

DORÉ: Jonathan. I want to tell Liana about my dream. *(To Liana)* Ever since I gave Jonathan up I still have a hard time saying it gave Jonathan up because I didn't really give him up he was pulled from my arms pulled from my /

MARCUS: That was a very long time ago.

DORÉ: That's just what I'm saying.

(As Doré tells about the tree she becomes more lively, less shy, and for some moments we see an energy in her we hadn't seen before. She does not rush the story, but rather tells it as though every sentence is connected to the whole.)

Ever since I was a girl a young girl of fifteen I dreamt night after night that I sat in the branches of a very large tree not afraid of the height no but of something else in the taller branches above me I can see its movement but not its shape I begin to climb up after it I have to know is it good or is it evil but just when I am close enough to grab its foot if it has a foot it falls I don't know if it's slipped or thrown itself. As it falls I reach out my hand and grab whatever I can and I got it I got it I'm so happy I forget to look at what I've got when I do look in my hand there is something small and wet and jelly and warm it's a piece of flesh and—

LIANA: How awful.

DORÉ: —I should be disgusted but I'm not I'm not then I feel a sudden pain in my thigh sudden I say though at the same moment I know it's been there all this time I lift my dress and there's a gash a wound the size of a lemon and then I just do it the most natural thing in the world I slide the piece of meat because that is what it now seems like into the wound in my thigh it fits perfectly it melds into me melts into me and the pain stops there's a lightness in me of my floating among the branches as the leaves do I don't come down 'til I wake.

(Silence some moments.)

LIANA: Wow. That's quite a dream.

DORÉ: But don't you see?

LIANA: See what?

DORÉ: In that tree above me what I've been climbing after all these years is Jonathan.

MARCUS: I think we should talk /

DORÉ *(Not hearing Marcus)*: But the most amazing thing isn't my actual dream it's when Jonathan first tells me he's been drawn to trees all his life.

(Liana looks at Marcus, who is uncomfortable.)

LIANA: You have?

(After a moment:)

MARCUS: Yes. I have.

LIANA: I. I didn't know. You never /

DORÉ: But that's how the two of you met you told me he was resting in a tree when you first saw him.

LIANA: No. He was leaning on a tree.

DORÉ: He was being carried up inside that tree. *(To Marcus)* Isn't that how you said it to me?

MARCUS: That's what it. Felt like, yes.

LIANA: Marcus. You were dozing against a tree. I was there, remember? I asked you what you were doing and you said:

MARCUS *(Smiles)*: "I was just having a little doze."

LIANA: Exactly. That's exactly what you said /

MARCUS: It doesn't really matter.

LIANA: It matters to me. Those were the first words you ever said to me: "I was just having a little doze." I cherish those words.

DORÉ: Maybe he was dozing but in his head he was climbing those branches and something down below something dark and warm and strong *(To Marcus)* that's how you described it is coming after you but you're afraid and keep on climbing even though you want to stop you ache to stop—

MARCUS: —to let it catch up with me—

DORÉ: —to let it devour you.

(Marcus looks straight at Doré for the first time in the scene.)

MARCUS: But I didn't have the courage.

(Doré smiles quickly at Marcus, then looks away.)

LIANA: So. Well.

(Doré suddenly deflates again and is shy.)

You both have a thing about trees.

DORÉ: I know it sounds silly.

MARCUS: Of course it does.

LIANA: It must be. It could be. Genetic. That you both are drawn—

DORÉ: Yes! Perhaps in the genes!

LIANA *(Continues)*: —to trees. Trees in your genes. The both of you.

DORÉ: Well, we are a family tree!

LIANA: And you've certainly put the tree into family in quite an original way!

MARCUS: Liana. Please don't mock.

LIANA: Darling. I'm not mocking. I'm.

DORÉ: Trying to understand Jonathan give her a chance there's bound to be some upset.

LIANA: Upset. I don't get upset about trees.

DORÉ: It was a maple in my dream it was never any other tree but a maple.

LIANA *(To Marcus)*: And your tree? Did you also dream of maples?

MARCUS: I never dreamed it. I just felt. It.

LIANA: So when you wanted to be "with" a tree, so to speak, did you seek out a maple?

MARCUS: I did.

LIANA: And all this time I thought a tree was just any old tree. Sorry. I'm mocking again, aren't I? *(To Doré)* Your tea is cold.

(Doré says her words all with the same weight:)

DORÉ: No worries cold tea wakes my mouth up don't you sometimes like it cold we're going to be living together from now on Jonathan and I he won't be coming home anymore after tonight to you.

LIANA: I could make a fresh pot if you like?

DORÉ: Please don't bother.

LIANA: It's no bother. Another slice of cake?

MARCUS: Doré. Why don't you wait in the car.

DORÉ: All right Jonathan.

LIANA *(To Marcus)*: Doré?

DORÉ: It can't be helped.

LIANA: In the summers I do enjoy a glass of cold tea. With ice and a lemon slice. *(To Marcus)* Don't we?

(Doré speaks hesitantly, repressing her excitement, but the words she uses, she tastes.)

DORÉ *(To Liana)*: I want to say forgive me but I feel the day black as it always was now has shapes and color /

MARCUS: Wait in the car. Please.

DORÉ *(To Liana)*: —balloons are nothing bells celebrations couldn't touch me but now in here—

(She lightly touches her chest.)

I feel so tall that if I straightened up I'd tear your roof off.

MARCUS: That's enough.

LIANA *(To Marcus)*: Darling, what is she saying?

(Silence. Marcus looks away.)

Marcus. Tell me what. What is she. You need to. *(Beat)* Marcus?

(Marcus won't look at Liana. Doré looks into her hands.)

Marcus?

(Suddenly Liana understands, with her gut more than her head. But it is as though this understanding is still very far away. There is a long, awkward silence.)

How did. Are you.

(Liana takes some moments to find her words.)

This. Did this. Happen?

MARCUS *(To Liana)*: We'll talk about it later.

(Liana is disorientated but composed.)

LIANA: How. Marcus?

DORÉ: It happened on the third night.

MARCUS: No. I will explain.

DORÉ: It was the third night he visited.

MARCUS: I will talk to her.

LIANA: Not the first night?

DORÉ: Nor the second. It was the third night.

(Liana takes this in. Silence some moments.)

LIANA: How did the. The first moment of it? Happen.

MARCUS *(To Liana)*: Don't. *(To Doré)* Go to the car, Doré.

(Doré makes a move to go, seeming small again. Liana's voice stops her.)

LIANA: Did you . . . How? . . . His hand a moment too long /

MARCUS: Don't do this. Please darling.

LIANA *(Calmly, to Marcus)*: Shut the fuck up.

DORÉ *(Firmly)*: Jonathan. Let her ask.

LIANA: How. Exactly did you. Seduce my husband?

(Doré tells the facts, with no gloating.)

DORÉ: My father was French he taught me how to make biscuits so light they float in your mouth and gravy like nectar there was stew I made stew and a light green salad I had gravy on my chin Jonathan wiped it away with his thumb such a tiny gesture I thought nothing of it then he slipped his thumb into my mouth /

MARCUS: Stop!

DORÉ *(Fact)*: She has a right to know.

MARCUS: The facts. A right to know the facts, nothing more.

DORÉ: But those are the facts. You put your thumb /

LIANA: Oh. I see. I see. *(Laughs with relief)* You are lying. Both of you are lying. This is a trick. Wow. A scam. What is it?

Huh? What is it? *(Beat)* The house! You want the house. You conniving bastard.

MARCUS: I don't want the house.

LIANA *(To Doré)*: He wants my house, doesn't he? To give it to you. To make up for.

DORÉ: I have my flat.

LIANA: That's it. Yes. That's it!

DORÉ: It's small but we'll make do.

LIANA *(To Doré)*: And money. I'm sure you want money. Who doesn't? *(To Marcus)* She's blackmailing you for money!

DORÉ: I have a little money of my own but /

LIANA: Exactly! When I visited you I offered to help you. How much do you want? *(To Marcus)* How much does she want?

DORÉ: Jonathan?

MARCUS: We don't want money.

LIANA: We. *(Beat)* Say it again.

MARCUS: We don't want money.

LIANA: We.

MARCUS: Yes.

(Liana is silent some moments. Then she begins to slowly say "no," over and over, sometimes with short beats between the "no"s, sometimes running them on. But there are no hysterics. Just firmness. She says "no" anywhere from twenty to thirty times. Marcus and Doré just listen.)

LIANA: No. No. No. No. No. No. No. No. No. No. No. No. No. No. No. No. No. No. No. No. No. No. No. No. No. No. No.

(Doré holds out her hand to Marcus and he moves to take it. They wait for Liana to stop.)

DORÉ: Yes.

(Liana regards them in silence for some moments, gathering herself.)

LIANA: Leaving aside that you're his mother, you are. An old woman. *(To Marcus)* She's an old woman.

(Doré looks away, shamed for a moment. Liana returns to the facts.)

The facts are. The facts are my husband is still in his prime. You are. Rotting.

MARCUS: Don't do this.

DORÉ: Shhh. Let her.

LIANA *(To Doré)*: You. You are certainly not. Sex! Sexy. Your skin is. Floppy. Your buttocks. Well. I have a tight ass—

(Liana smacks her own ass hard.)

—like I did when I was twenty. When you have a good laugh you probably leak urine in your panties. Yes. That's what happens when the body ages. My own mother wore pads from the age of fifty-one. Do you wear pads, Doré? For that unexpected leakage?

(Doré looks away.)

Whatever insanity you are stirring up here, you should know that Marcus still wants me. Yes he does. And right now he's got the smell of my pussy on his fingers.

MARCUS: Oh Jesus . . .

LIANA *(Triumphantly)*: He made me cum just minutes before you arrived.

DORÉ *(To Marcus)*: Did you? *(Beat)* Well, I've always thought a good fingering before any stressful event makes a woman more relaxed, more able to take it all in.

LIANA: You are. Sick.

DORÉ: We all have our own way of saying good-bye.

LIANA: Get out of my house or we'll call the police.

(Liana goes to stand by Marcus, takes his hand. At first it seems he responds. He grips Liana's hand tight. Then he slowly pulls away. Liana takes this in for some moments.)

(To Marcus) I will never believe this. Never.

(Silence between the three of them. Marcus looks away. Doré slowly approaches Marcus and speaks to him. It is difficult for her to put herself forward but she makes herself do it.)

DORÉ *(Kindly)*: Do you still love your wife, Jonathan, your sad beautiful wife?

MARCUS: Yes, I do.

LIANA: There. Those are the facts. Ha. He loves me. Fact.

DORÉ: Then you must free her from you. From us.

(Marcus just looks back at Doré, completely present with her.)

You owe her. If you still care for Liana don't leave her with hope.

(Marcus nods slightly, then kisses Doré, lightly at first, then more deeply, and she responds. He envelops her in his arms like a lover. It is a quiet, focused moment of passion, restrained but therefore the desire all the more evident. Liana watches them, frozen, mesmerized. She watches long enough until all doubt is erased and the image of their embrace is burned into her mind and body. Then Liana turns slowly away, quietly, striving for dignity. The only sign of her near collapse is a brief moment when her knees give way. But she catches herself immediately.)

Marcus and Doré break off their kiss, not forgetting where they are but still in the privacy of their passion. Doré glances at Liana's back, then leaves quietly. Marcus watches her go. When he turns back around, Liana has turned around also. They look at each other some long, painful, and on Liana's part, angry moments. She attempts to suppress her emotions.)

LIANA: I. *(Beat)* I.

(Silence.)

You. *(Beat)* We . . .

(Silence as Liana contains herself, trying to regain control.)

What will we. Tell Dominique?

MARCUS: I don't know.

LIANA: Have you molested her?

MARCUS: Christ no. Jesus, how could you— No, no!

LIANA *(Convinced)*: I believe you. *(Beat)* We'll tell Dom we're getting a divorce. It will be hard for her but better than.

MARCUS: Yes, a divorce.

LIANA: Not an ugly divorce. But a quiet. Considerate divorce. No need for her to fret. Civil. Liberating for the both of us.

MARCUS: She'll like that word, "liberating" . . .

LIANA: She will. I'll say that we were. "Oppressed" by our many years of. Familiarity.

MARCUS: Divergence of interests.

LIANA: Yes. That's better. Oppressed by our divergence of interests. It's common.

MARCUS: That's right. So many of our friends, their marriages have stalled. Gone stale. We're not any different.

LIANA: Not at all. Middle-age crisis. And mutual. *(Practicing)* "It's all mutual, Dom. It's even . . . exciting."

MARCUS: "We're excited about our new lives."

LIANA: Yes. I think I can say that to her.

MARCUS: And that we'll remain friends.

LIANA: Not that.

MARCUS: Then she won't believe us.

LIANA: We'll say we need a complete . . . severing. So that new . . . shoots can spring up.

MARCUS: A severing. *(Beat)* All right. For the new shoots.

LIANA: I'll tell my friends the same. My clients. My boss. I will put a spring in my step. My coworkers will say, "Look at her. Wow. That's what divorce will do for you." I'll say, "I'm looking forward to being single again after so many years." But Dom is so sensitive. What if she suspects?

MARCUS: We can't let her.

LIANA: No. *(Beat)* I will never say, "Dominique. My darling. Your father never kissed me with such. Abandon." I will never say, "Dominique, my only child, my treasure, when he kissed her I could see his cock hard through his trousers."

(Marcus starts to speak. Liana silences him.)

No. No! *(Beat)* Dom would ask me, she always asks. She is so blunt: "Who? Who?" Though now she'll be weeping. Weeping as I've never heard her weep, even as a child. "Who was it you saw Father kissing?" She'll be standing on a street corner in Chicago, the dirty snow puddled at her feet, crushing the phone to her cold winter ear, the traffic swearing all around her so it makes it difficult for her to hear me. And when I answer, when I say, "His mother," three thousand seven hundred miles away, on the other side of the ocean, there will be a sound neither of us will hear. A "crack," almost imperceptible. And like a clear glass ornament, our daughter's heart will drop from her small body and hit the pavement.

(Silence some moments.)

MARCUS: Don't tell her. I beg you.

LIANA *(Firm)*: You're going to lose everything. I'll make sure.

MARCUS: Liana.

LIANA: Don't say my name again.

MARCUS: This is not about us. This is not about. Let me try and explain /

LIANA: Don't! Don't you dare. Use. Words. To try and. To make me, understand. I will never.

MARCUS: Please. Just let me . . . *(Beat)* I've done some. Investigating.

LIANA: Investigating. Ah.

MARCUS: And it turns out that it's more common than you think. *(Beat)* GSA. Than we think. Genetic Sexual Attraction.

LIANA: Oh? So there's a name for it. Genetic Sexual Attraction. Well what do you know? That draws a line under it then.

MARCUS *(Facts)*: There's very little written on it in academic circles. This. This phenomenon. But the few post-adoption experts say—

LIANA: Experts?

MARCUS *(Facts)*: That this . . . occurs. That this. Genetic attraction. Occurs in over half of these reunions. Some believe almost as many may act on this . . . On this . . .

LIANA: Phenomenon . . .

MARCUS *(Facts)*: Yes. When meeting for a first time. That a subconscious memory, even the smell of one's own. Family. Can cause an acute physical reaction. An urge for intimacy that sometimes becomes . . .

LIANA: Incest?

MARCUS: No! *(Beat)* The same experts distinguish GSA from. That, as there's no force, no coercion. No victim.

LIANA *(Flatly)*: No victim . . .

MARCUS: In fact, it's a largely normal response to an extremely unusual situation.

(A moment of silence while Liana seems to take this in.)

LIANA: GSA . . . Though I'm not sure that it's more precise than SFM, Son Fucks Mother. Or MFS, Mother Fucks Son.

MARCUS: This I won't do. No /

LIANA: Oh yes you will. You will answer every fucking question I ask you or I'll phone our daughter right now. Right now! *(Beat)* You owe me. *(Getting control again)* Do you sit in her lap and suck your thumb?

MARCUS: No.

LIANA: I read that once somewhere. Do you wear a diaper and shit, so she can clean you up?

MARCUS: Of course not.

LIANA: Sprinkle your bottom with talcum powder?

MARCUS: No.

LIANA: GSA. Genetic Sexual Attraction. The first time on top of her or under?

(Marcus hesitates only a moment.)

MARCUS: On top.

LIANA: Was your tongue in her mouth when you came? *(Quiet, threatening)* Answer me.

MARCUS: Yes.

LIANA: You used to do that with me. But . . . *(Sings a line from Barbra Streisand)* "You don't bring me flowers anymore." When we were youthful. Radiant.

MARCUS: We'll talk about this later. I should go.

LIANA *(Firmly)*: You. Will. Go. When. I. Am. Finished. These last moments are mine. *(Beat)* We have a life other people

envy. A beautiful child. We have more sex than teenag-
ers do. We both love seventeenth-century Dutch paint-
ers and we've seen two of Dürer's self-portraits together.
We were going to Madrid next spring to see the third.
We travel well. We listen to one another. Laugh at each
other's jokes. Why? Why?

MARCUS: I don't know if I can. Explain in a way that makes
sense or. Translates into.

LIANA: Give it a go.

MARCUS: The head or the brain, it's not a part of that, so there's
no "why" I can talk about. When she opened the door and
I saw her face it was like looking at someone I'd been looking at all my life but never seen. We didn't embrace. She
held out her hand and I took it. And that simple contact.

(Marcus falters.)

LIANA: Yes?

MARCUS: Just the skin of her hand to my hand. That contact.
It was. It was.

(He falters again.)

LIANA *(Quietly)*: I'm listening.

MARCUS: Unbearable. Necessary. In another time and yet so
firmly rooted in that moment I felt for the first time fully
alive. In agony yes, but fully alive.

*(Liana feels a moment of intense physical weakness but quickly
steadies herself.)*

LIANA: Well who could compete with that?

MARCUS: I'm not explaining it correctly. Saying it the way I. If
I could /

LIANA: I'm quite sure I can say that I have not felt such an intense sensation, ever. No. Not even with you. The birth of Dominique was. Fierce. When her head crowned, I felt a. Force tear through me I thought would rip me in half but I've never felt what you. *(Beat)* Do you long for her? Don't lie.

MARCUS: Every moment.

LIANA: Even when you had your fingers inside me just an hour ago?

(Marcus nods.)

Why did you touch me if you were going to leave?

MARCUS: You're the most brilliant woman /

LIANA: Fuck brilliant. We're talking desire, lascivious need.

MARCUS: There is something about you that is always. Gone. I've never grown tired of trying to find it.

LIANA: But you don't want me like you want her?

MARCUS: It's different.

LIANA: How is it different?

(Marcus just shakes his head.)

Or is it just the taste that's different? *(Beat)* Did you go down on her?

MARCUS: Jesus, Liana.

LIANA: Let me rephrase: Have you licked your mother's cunt?

(Marcus is suddenly enraged and furiously kicks one of the chairs over. We have no warning that this rage will erupt. It seems to come out of nowhere, and then disappears just as quickly. Silence between them.)

All right. We'll let that one go. Allow for a little mystery here.

(Marcus rights the chair, checking to see he hasn't broken it.)

I wish I could believe that you are insane. I could try and believe that.

MARCUS: I know it doesn't make sense, Liana. Even to me. But wanting her /

LIANA: Say "my mother." I want to hear it.

MARCUS: Wanting my. Mother. I'm filled with. Rope.

LIANA: Rope? Well, isn't that novel.

MARCUS: Rope. Yes. And there's no room left inside me. Filled with it, tangled, knotted, packed so tight my skin will burst and one touch from her. She takes the small end of all that mass and begins to pull, to wind me out of myself and it hurts like fucking hell but it feels perfect and unmitigated, exactly what I need until I'm pooled at her feet, miles and miles of me pooled at her feet and me still standing there. Utterly emptied. And utterly.

LIANA: Complete?

(Quiet some moments.)

I don't think I've ever felt that either. Though I'm not sure I'd want to because then it's game over, isn't it? *(Beat)* You know what was the best part for me all these years? Monday through Friday when I come home you've already finished up in Skipton, at the school, and you get here first. Fifteen, twenty years it's been like this and in all this time I've never tired of it. I ring the bell and you come to the door and open it and greet me when I get home. That moment when the door swings open and I see your face. Refreshing like a mint or a wedge of orange. Why do you always want to open the door for me? I've wondered many times but never asked. I suppose I was afraid that if I asked, you'd stop. Most couples use their own key. Only strangers ring the bell. No one waits at the door. But you are always. Were always there as I crossed the threshold.

MARCUS: Doré is waiting in the car. It's started to rain.

(Liana looks at the window.)

LIANA: We were never bothered by rain, you and I. Just a few weeks ago, I think, it was the first of November. No, it was the second because it was the day before Dominique's twenty-first birthday and we stood in that window. Together. And listened to the rain.

MARCUS: Yes we did.

LIANA *(Facts)*: Everything. You have ruined. But my heart, now a filthy, contaminated bear cage, when I have finished will be pounded clean, sterilized with a fire hose. Nothing inside of me will remain of you. *(Beat)* Give it to me.

MARCUS: What?

LIANA: What? What? What? What?

MARCUS: I don't under /

LIANA: What the hell do you think I'm asking for? The receipt! You were going to pick up our winter blanket at the dry cleaner's on Monday. You won't be doing that now, will you?

(Marcus takes out his wallet, slowly searches, finds the receipt, gives it to her. Liana almost unconsciously caresses the receipt. At some point she'll put it in her pocket.)

MARCUS: And now that this is done /

LIANA: "This"?

MARCUS: Yes. Now that this is done, I want you to ask me. *(Beat)* Go on.

LIANA: Ask you what?

MARCUS: Something you might have asked a few weeks ago.

LIANA: What?

MARCUS: "Marcus. My love. My husband. My life's companion. I've got an idea. A rousing idea! How would you like to meet your mother, for the very first time, for your fortieth birthday?" Because really, Liana, one should ask, don't you think? It's not quite the same as, "Would you like a new scarf for your birthday? Black perhaps? Or dark green, in cashmere?"

(Liana just looks at him.)

Why didn't you ask me?

LIANA: It was a surprise.

MARCUS: I've had her address for twelve years.

(Liana is startled.)

LIANA: What?

MARCUS: Yes. Twelve years. But I never contacted her.

LIANA: You never told me . . .

MARCUS *(Ignoring her)*: I didn't want any more than that. It was enough to know that she was. Alive. That she was out there somewhere.

LIANA: Wait a minute. Don't you dare try to blame me /

(Suddenly Marcus picks up a fork from the tray. He pulls back Liana's blouse and holds the fork to her heart, dangerously, letting it push at her skin.)

MARCUS: You conniving, ignorant bitch . . .

(Liana is surprised but she doesn't struggle.)

LIANA: A fork? There's a knife lying right next to it. Why don't you pick up the knife?

MARCUS: A fork will make an uglier hole. I've got the strength for it. You know that.

(Liana is quiet a moment, then:)

LIANA: I dare you. Jonathan.

(Marcus raises his arm suddenly, as though to strike at Liana's heart. There is violence in his voice.)

MARCUS: You. Never. Asked me.

(Liana touches his cheek with one finger, sensually, briefly.)

LIANA: Feel that? The last time I'll touch you. I won't ever do so again. Not if a gun were held to my temple. Or my child's.

(Marcus suddenly lets Liana go. He puts the fork back neatly on the tray. He moves to leave.)

Before you disappear into your. Trees forever. We should conclude with a few parting words.

(Marcus waits, his back to her. Liana, briefly, almost unconsciously, rubs her chest where the fork touched her skin; she is bruised.)

How about . . . "Go to hell" or "Forgive me"? Or that old standard "I hope you drop dead"?

MARCUS: We could just say good-bye.

LIANA: Too mundane.

(Liana thinks. Marcus turns and watches her.)

How about I stand here. As though I've just got home and it's late afternoon, almost dark. Winter is coming fast. And then you say to me what you've said to me for twenty years. And then you leave. And I won't open my eyes again until you're gone.

MARCUS: Liana.

LIANA: Pay attention. *(Beat)* I'm closing my eyes. There. I've just rung the bell. I'm tired. My scarf has slipped and the wind is cold on my neck. I'm so glad to get home. To unwind. I hear your footsteps in the hall, quick, quick. You never let me wait! You open the door. We look at each other, and you say:

(A moment of silence, then Marcus answers:)

MARCUS: "My darling. How was your day?"

(Liana stands still, eyes remaining closed. A slight smile on her lips, remembering. Marcus goes. After some long moments Liana slowly opens her eyes. The smile fades. She looks out into a new distance. As though she can see herself, far away, standing on an empty horizon.)

ACT THREE

Six years later.

> *Lights up on a small bare room off the side of a church chapel. There is a plain rough-wood coffin. Doré is standing, calmly looking at the coffin. Strangely, Doré looks more youthful, even taller. She is elegant, fashionably though subtly dressed in black. And black becomes her. Doré lets her hand rest lightly on the coffin. She circles it, letting her hand run down its length. She winces when she gets a splinter. Doré tries to squeeze it out, then sucks on her finger to try and draw the splinter out. She gives up and just stares at the coffin again. Liana enters, but stays near the edge. She watches Doré's back, which is to her. Liana looks to have aged beyond her years and has a slight limp. Her hair is tied back from her face. She is not dressed in black. Though her clothes are worn, they still retain a sense of flair. Liana carries an old leather suitcase. Doré senses someone enter. At first she does not turn around.*

DORÉ: Hello Liana.

(A long pause. Liana sets down the suitcase. She glances at the coffin. She doesn't want to give it attention but she can't help the glancing.)

Not much of a crowd, was it? Six in total, if you count the priest. And I do.

LIANA: What happened?

(Doré turns around. She looks Liana in the eye. Doré's shyness is gone, replaced by a calm steadfastness. Most of the time, Doré no longer speaks in unbroken sentences.)

DORÉ: He died.

LIANA: Cancer?

DORÉ: How are you?

LIANA *(Hopeful)*: Testicular? Prostate?

(Doré doesn't reply. Liana can't help approaching the coffin. Liana reaches to touch the wood, but doesn't. She withdraws her hand as though burned.)

DORÉ: Not much more than a crate, is it? Rough. Simple.

LIANA: Cheap.

DORÉ: It's as he wished.

LIANA: He wanted to be cremated.

DORÉ: It's a woodland burial for him now. Tomorrow we'll put him in the ground. There are some lovely woods a few miles from here, with a wide range of wildflowers. Sorrel, bluebells. Squill. We used to walk there together on Satur /

LIANA: Trees.

DORÉ: Sorry?

LIANA: To be close to the trees.

DORÉ: Oh. Well. Neither of us ever thought much about trees again after we'd— Your feet are wet.

LIANA (*Looking at her feet*): I stood outside during the service.

DORÉ: In the rain? (*Beat*) You've gone grey.

(*Liana touches her hair briefly.*)

Once quite beautiful. Elegant too. We were sorry to hear you lost your job.

LIANA: That was a good while ago.

DORÉ: You were fired.

LIANA: Wrong. I quit. I didn't give a damn what my insufferable colleagues thought but all that excited whispering trying to pass itself off as silent indifference killed my creative urge. (*Beat*) I never told anyone but news travels quick. Stink even quicker. My daughter discovered it from the internet, on some obscure Chicago social network site for young artists.

DORÉ: Where do you live now?

LIANA: Live?

DORÉ: Where do you sleep?

LIANA: Sleep I find a waste of time, but in small doses, I submit.

DORÉ: I haven't slept properly for years. With Marcus in the /

LIANA: Marcus?

DORÉ: Yes.

LIANA: But he's Jonathan to you.

DORÉ: He was, yes, but after a while he preferred Marcus again. But when I was angry with him I'd still call him Jonathan!

LIANA: You were telling me about trees.

DORÉ: I was telling you about sleep. How he could sleep! Not a care in the world. He had this funny sound

(*Liana looks away.*)

when he slept. Like a—

LIANA: —whistle.

DORÉ: Perhaps more like a tune. From his chest.

LIANA: It started after he got pneumonia when he was twenty-seven.

DORÉ: He said it was from smoking.

LIANA: He never smoked.

DORÉ: On holidays we'd share a cigarette or two. Just for the taste. *(Beat)* Well, that little tune from his chest—as though it were stuck on one note. Precious. I couldn't help but stay awake to listen to it. He didn't know I often watched him sleep.

LIANA: He was fired from his teaching job.

DORÉ: Not exactly. He quit before they could fire him.

LIANA: He loved that job. He said his students renewed him, gave him conviction.

DORÉ: Oh he hated those girls. Called them his "little bitches." He set up his own business: tutorials online, prep for university, that sort of thing. Students from all over the world. He earned more than he did at the high school and he could do the work from home. He asked me to give up my cleaning job, that way we could be at home togeth /

LIANA: So you didn't come home from work anymore. He didn't greet you at the door.

DORÉ: There was no need; I was already there. *(Beat)* I saw Dominique at the service.

LIANA: She's hard to miss.

DORÉ: She looks like you. Once did.

LIANA: We've spent the morning at the Henry Moore Institute. She's flying back to Chicago tonight. Lots of new work to make for a show in the spring, March.

DORÉ: Got her foot on the wheel!

LIANA: It's a series, in bright colors, of old, brick chimneys.

DORÉ: I've always loved old chimneys.

LIANA: Chimneys in ruins, broken off midway up, collapsed on their roofs. *(Beat)* She's beginning to get some notice. She'll make her mark. *(Glancing at the coffin again)* Was it suicide?

DORÉ: What does your daughter think of her mum living in a bedsit? Surviving on benefits?

LIANA: These days, unless you're eating rabbits off the road or can demonstrate, right there in the office, that you make a hot cuppa every morning with small, measured spoons of your cat's excrement, you won't get any benefits. I did try, though. Then I got a fork stuck in my leg.

DORÉ: How on earth did that happen?

LIANA: I gripped it like a knife and I stuck it in.

DORÉ: On purpose?

LIANA: It's hard to do if it's not on purpose.

DORÉ: But why?

LIANA: Why do you suppose?

DORÉ: Because you were. Anguished?

LIANA: Anguished. Your vocabulary has certainly improved. Well, that's what comes from living with a teacher for six years. But anguish is elegant and for elegance one uses a knife; deep and smooth. However, when your insides have rearranged themselves and are now hanging on your outside, I recommend a fork. There's no pretense with a fork. *(Beat)* A more practical reason was to apply for sympathy.

DORÉ: Did you get it?

LIANA: No. Just a damnable infection and a limp.

DORÉ: I'm sorr /

LIANA: I knew it would happen: suicide. To either of you, or both. In the first couple of years, I would see you hanging by the neck from that broken tree in your yard, that he would find you there, your tongue thick and gray, your legs dripping with shit from your convulsions. I like that detail. Then I would imagine him slitting his wrists, sinking to the bedroom floor. Your face when you find him there. I imagined the day, the time, what socks he'd be wearing. The silver clips in your hair. Hours of it. It was my job and I excelled. It was far more exciting than advertising. Arousing even. Then one day my head got bored with the same old routine and began to taunt me. The blood would turn to orange; it wouldn't stay red. Or the blade he'd use to cut his wrists would turn to wool. *(Beat)* Tell me how he killed himself.

DORÉ: You came here alone. Is there no one special in your life?

(Liana just looks away.)

You're not old yet, Liana. If you made a little effort, if you spruced, you might surely have a date now and then?

LIANA: I don't like dates. But give me a bag of apricots and they'll be down the hatch in two.

DORÉ: My dear, I meant /

LIANA *(Flatly)*: I know what you meant and stay the fuck out of my life.

(Doré glances at the suitcase.)

DORÉ: You're going away?

LIANA: Yes. In a manner: I'm moving house.

DORÉ: Ah. Adventure. I've lived in my flat for forty-one years. Perhaps I should have wanted for something else, somewhere else but I never did. I know every groan and squeak of the stairs, the soft click of the cupboards, the snap of each light switch. With the flat so quiet again, their chatterings have come back to me like comfortable old friends.

LIANA: Do you like to travel?

DORÉ: I like to be in my home. I've enough good memories now.

LIANA: I'm going to give you something.

DORÉ: Oh. There's no need.

LIANA: Yes there is.

DORÉ: Well. What are you going to give me?

LIANA: Twenty-four hours.

DORÉ: Twenty-four hours? What for?

LIANA: To get out of my flat.

DORÉ: Your flat?

LIANA: No. I'll give you until tomorrow morning. Say nine A.M.?

(Doré laughs.)

Marcus left your home to me.

DORÉ: What?

LIANA: I too was surprised but I've been notified.

DORÉ: That's not possible.

LIANA: You put the flat in his name.

DORÉ: When I stopped working, yes, naturally I couldn't pay the mortgage any longer . . .

LIANA: And naturally he expected you to die first so the house you gave to him he left, in his will, to Dom and me. Do you think it was his way of telling Dominique he was sorry?

DORÉ: Jonathan was never sorry.

LIANA: Let's say that by seven A.M. you've skedaddled from the flat. If not, I will hire a couple of tired, angry, sour-smelling men with big idle hands, from my building, for just a few bottles of cheap cider, and they will come over and toss you out. You'll have to start work again. Without skills, you'll soon be back to sticking your face in some sloppy teenager's toilet bowl. I'm looking forward to lighting a fire on cold nights.

DORÉ: We filled the fireplace with bricks.

LIANA: Is the flat still crammed with that '70s junk?

DORÉ: My father sang to me every day when I was a child, old French nursery rhymes. I was nineteen when he settled me into the flat and set up my mortgage for me. Then he and my mother moved South, as far away as they could get without crossing the water /

LIANA: I'm going to ask these same men to collect every stick of furniture you leave behind; they can sell it on or dump it in a skip. Then I'm going to repaint the rooms, myself. All the crockery out too. Every cup and mug and spoon your mouth touched. His touched. Out. I'll start again. You'll have to start again.

DORÉ: There's no such thing.

LIANA: It's cold and brutal to be without a roof. Enjoy.

DORÉ: I loved Marcus completely. You can't touch that.

LIANA: Completely. That's a tall order. He once spoke of needing that. I admit I don't know what it means; to love someone completely. I once cared for Marcus as well. And I say "cared," because care is the wayward cousin of love, dogged, in need of redecorating, but a little less shrill around the edges. Did I care for him completely? No. Because I never cared for his feet.

(Liana gives a small shiver. Silence some moments.)

DORÉ: Neither did I.

LIANA: He gave his feet too much attention.

DORÉ: Yes he did, as though they were . . . pets. *(Beat)* We shouldn't talk like this.

LIANA: And why not? To love someone absolutely is a disrespect. Always hold something back: a little piece of aversion keeps one inquisitive, cognizant.

DORÉ: I didn't have an aversion to his feet. I just couldn't feel friendly towards them. They were too clean.

LIANA: Clean the way feet shouldn't be, and pink and moist.

DORÉ: The nails trimmed straight across, no curve!

LIANA: And his particularity with socks!

DORÉ: No synthetics.

LIANA AND DORÉ: All cotton only.

DORÉ: So his feet could breathe.

LIANA: Permissible was a mix of cashmere and cotton in winter. Preferably organic material.

DORÉ: And socks turned inside out in the wash so they'd be perfectly clean.

LIANA: To love one's own feet with such diligence, such zeal.

DORÉ: It's suspect.

LIANA: Always glancing down to make sure they were still there—

DORÉ: As though they were two holy relics. Sometimes it seemed they actually glowed in the dark!

(The two women burst out laughing together for some moments, almost giggling, forgetting themselves. Then suddenly Liana's hands are tight around Doré's throat. Doré does not resist, just looks Liana in the eye.)

I didn't fancy his favorite oldie either. You must know his favorite song?

(Doré begins to sing "Sittin' On the Dock of the Bay." She does the whistle as well. Liana grips tighter, but slowly, and Doré begins to have trouble singing the song. Doré does not try to stop Liana. The choking goes on for some time and the song is slowly choked out of Doré, until only a few small noises, like ugly notes, escape her. Doré begins to sink to her knees. At the end, Doré naturally fights for her life. Then Doré slumps, seemingly unconscious, on the floor and Liana releases her and

steps away. She just stares at Doré's crumpled body for some moments. Then she glances around her: What has she done?)

LIANA: Doré.

(Liana prods Doré's body with her shoe. No response.)

Doré? *(Beat)* Fucking hell, Liana.

(Liana grabs her suitcase to leave. Doré does not move or open her eyes when she speaks.)

DORÉ: Am I. Dead?

(Liana starts.)

LIANA: My God. What have I done to be so, so—
DORÉ: I think I'm all right.
LIANA: —disappointed at every turn.

(Doré opens her eyes, though still not moving a muscle.)

DORÉ: You tried to kill me.

(Liana answers as though she were saying: "Of course I didn't.")

LIANA: Of course I did. *(Beat)* Get off the floor.
DORÉ: I like it down here. It's warm.

(Dore wipes some tears from her eyes, though we haven't seen her cry.)

LIANA: Someone will come. You'll embarrass both of us. Get up.
DORÉ: Oh, oh. That's why it felt so warm. I've pissed myself.

(Liana does not move to help her. Doré slowly gets to her feet, and not easily. Liana makes a sound of disgust.)

LIANA: I cannot bear you.
DORÉ: Well I was being strangled after all. I do hope you got that out of your system.

(Doré finds some tissues in her pocket and dries the floor.)

Did you know that Marcus wrote to his daughter for years?

(Liana moves further away from the small puddle on the floor.)

LIANA: She told me.
DORÉ: Did she read the letters?
LIANA: She would call me from Chicago each time she got one and ask me to stay on the phone while she ground it in the garbage disposal.
DORÉ: He longed for Dominique. Like there was no tomorrow.
LIANA: And now there isn't, for him.
DORÉ: I approached Dom after the /
LIANA: Dominique. Only family says "Dom."
DORÉ: I said to her, "He always hoped to see you again." She smiled at me. Just a little quick smile but it was something.

(Liana nods, but she doesn't believe her. Doré feels uncomfortable in her wet skirt.)

Ugh. Do you have an extra tissue so I can dry myself?

(As Liana says the following, she almost unconsciously takes the cotton scarf from around her neck and gives it to Doré.)

LIANA: No. And if I did I wouldn't give it to you.

(Doré takes the scarf and, quickly and modestly as she can, wipes herself dry, then finishes up the floor.)

DORÉ: I haven't pissed myself in years, always had a bladder tight as a jar. *(Beat)* I'll be out of the flat in three days. Give me that much time, please. There's a lot to pack up.

(Doré doesn't know what to do with the scarf after she's used it.)

LIANA: Forty-eight hours and no more.
DORÉ: Thank you.

(Finally Doré drapes the scarf on the end of the coffin.)

I'll just leave it there to dry.

(Doré moves to leave.)

LIANA: Wait. A minute. I—

(Liana opens her suitcase. Inside are a few pieces of clothing, books, photos. She frantically searches and then finds some underwear.)

You should change. Before you go.

(Doré is unsure. Liana dangles the underwear from her finger. A moment of silence.)

DORÉ: Those are not very attractive.
LIANA: They're clean.

(Doré takes the panties and quickly but discreetly changes into the clean ones behind the coffin.)

DORÉ: He won't mind my changing here. He'd just laugh.

LIANA: I remember his voice, and the sound of him moving in the next room. But not his laugh.

DORÉ: It was a very low laugh, sort of gutty.

LIANA: You mean "guttural."

(Doré comes out from behind the coffin.)

DORÉ: Yes, that's what I mean. A bit like . . .

(Doré tries Marcus's laugh. She doesn't do a very good job.)

LIANA: When I first met you, you tried a snort. It wasn't a very good snort either. And that is not Marcus's laugh.

DORÉ: This is the first time I've tried it.

(Doré tries to make Marcus's laugh again. And fails again. Liana shakes her head no. Then Doré adjusts her body, her legs, her arms, taking her time, to make herself into Marcus's body. This time the laugh is Marcus's. She laughs and laughs Marcus's laugh. Liana does not join in. Doré quits.)

He missed you, Liana.

LIANA: Don't. Don't you dare.

(For the first time here we see Liana's pent-up anguish.)

Shut the fuck up. Shut the fuck up!

(Silence. The women just look at one another. Even Liana is surprised by her own outburst. Then Liana speaks calmly, directly:)

How do you know he missed me?

DORÉ: He said, "I miss her."

LIANA: You lying bitch. You scum! *(Beat)* How do you know he meant me? He could have meant Dom. Did he say my name?

DORÉ: No. But the only her to him, to us, was you. He said

LIANA: "I miss her?"

DORÉ: And I said: "If you ever say that again . . . " And I gave him a look.

LIANA: And he never said it again?

DORÉ: Once was enough. We both knew that.

LIANA: So you weren't always happy together.

DORÉ: Happy. Does loving Dominique make you happy?

(Liana thinks about the question a moment.)

LIANA: Every minute, especially when it's going well, I'm terrified for her.

DORÉ: So you see.

LIANA: No I don't.

DORÉ: We were so finely etched he and I so finely carved that's the word he used from the same stone.

LIANA: Carved.

DORÉ: From a single block and when we first came together we were one thing again whole but the desire it was so bright /

LIANA: Please, don't.

DORÉ: We had to close our eyes when we made love /

LIANA: Stop. Not that, no.

DORÉ: But, Liana, I want you to know. With that kind of heat, well, it began to corrode us that's the word Marcus used corrode my arm that was his arm became mine again his thigh that was my thigh became his again our shapes began to reappear, untangling, and our single block became two bodies again we lost the strength of our grappling and could only lay side by side.

(Liana takes this in.)

LIANA: So in a nutshell, as time passed he no longer wanted to fuck you? Excellent. Blue-chip. And how did that feel?

DORÉ: I was fifteen when he was pulled from my arms.

LIANA: I was forty-three.

DORÉ: It's not the same thing. I was a child. Just a girl when I got pregna /

LIANA: Of course. Marvelous. Just let it all out why don't you? Don't tell me: a mean old uncle with a mouth full of pork pie and brandy, groped you. But wait. Maybe it was your father. Of course. Therefore the furniture; you were abused by your dear old daddio.

(Doré just stares at Liana, then shakes her head no.)

To be perfectly honest, Doré, I don't care if Santa Claus gave you a brand new pink teddy with one hand while he fingered you to the tune of "Jingle Bells" with the other. Before, of course, giving you a good shagging inside a fake igloo, surrounded by plastic reindeer.

DORÉ *(Facts)*: Marcus's father was an exquisite boy of seventeen. His family were travelers and they were passing through town. I kissed him first. We made love with such tenderness I thought it was a dream. The next day his family moved on, and he was gone. *(Beat)* My mother and father never forgave me for giving myself to a traveler. *(Beat)* Most of my life it seemed anyone could look right through me. Transparent, the only mark I could make was a finger 'cross a frosty window pane.

LIANA: What a charming way to put it.

DORÉ: Rain fell through me not on me.

LIANA: Don't forget to mention the snow.

DORÉ: When my name was called it hardly made a sound but you, look at you Liana. You were like a stallion when I first met you sparks at your heels as you walked always moving orchestrating as you called it, bursting with the world you carried with you /

LIANA: That's right, and you were just a body washed up on shore until Marcus gave you the kiss of life.

DORÉ: I too believed his love made me formidable. But then came the disappointment.

LIANA: So you got what you wanted and you're still an ungrateful whore.

DORÉ: Look at you. I who couldn't do a thing with my life but slump down inside it. You've been torn apart you've been pulled inside out like an old gray sock and then folded the wrong way who did this? Who did this? Not Marcus. I did this to you. I changed you. Without even touching the pigments I created a work of art /

LIANA: You've been practicing that little ditty for years, haven't you?

(Doré is silent. She looks away. A little of her old shyness returns.)

DORÉ: A few days before he died he came to my bed again /

LIANA: Christ.

DORÉ: We no longer slept in the same room. It had been almost two years. That night /

LIANA: I no longer have any curiosity about these details. I've made peace with the fact—

DORÉ: But I want to tell you.

LIANA: —that each of us is born with the smear of our mother's cunt across our faces and we carry it with us all our lives. A very, very few of us go back for more, that's all.

DORÉ *(Shouts for the first time)*: Shut up, Liana. For God's sake shut up and listen that's the one thing you've never learned how to do or get the hell out. You came here this is my world!

(Liana is taken aback by Doré's outburst and is silenced. Doré continues, composed again.)

We no longer slept in the same room. It had been almost two years. That night we lay together our bodies touching but not using our hands. There was no arousal. Our skin was between us like cool water. He lay his head on my chest and for the first time he was truly my son again. And I his mother. We lay like that all night, our skin circulating back and forth between us like liquid. Three days later he was dead. His death was not a suicide. He died of an aneurysm.

LIANA: An aneurysm?!

DORÉ: Yes.

LIANA: No.

DORÉ: Yes.

LIANA: You mean he didn't even know he died?

DORÉ: That quick.

LIANA: He didn't suffer?

DORÉ: Not a minute.

LIANA: He didn't call out?

DORÉ: Not a sound. He was buttering a crumpet, then he collapsed.

LIANA *(Fact)*: A crumpet.

DORÉ: One could not ask for a more gentle way to go.

LIANA: The bastard.

(A silence.)

DORÉ: The way things happened between Marcus and I was not the way it was supposed to happen but how they ended up was where we had to be. I don't think we could have got there any other way. What I'm trying to say, Liana, is: I am sor /

LIANA: No. This is all . . . It just can't be that . . . I don't believe you . . .

(Liana stares at the coffin.)

Anyone. There could be anyone in that coffin. You could be making this all up.

DORÉ: What? *(Beat)* Oh. No, Liana. Marcus is dead.

LIANA: Is he? Is he truly dead and gone? I think I should have a look, just to be sure.

DORÉ: The viewing was a few hours ago. The lid's been sealed.

LIANA: Then I'll unseal it.

(Liana approaches the coffin. She reaches to unlatch the upper part of the box. It's sealed. Liana takes off her shoe. She uses it to bash open the hinges. Liana's hands are shaking. We see now that Liana is suddenly so afraid that she's having trouble breathing. She lifts the lid an inch, then sets it back down again: she can't do it. She moves away from the coffin. She doesn't cry but rather moans, as though in physical pain, sick. Like a child she crouches into herself. Doré just watches her for some time, then:)

DORÉ: Would you like me to open the coffin for you?

(Liana shakes her head no.)

Yes. That's what I'll do. I'll open it up for you so you can see that /

LIANA: No. No! Don't open it! Don't. Please. It's empty. Don't you see? It will be empty!

DORÉ: But it's not empty /

(Liana now releases the anger and sorrow she's been holding back.)

LIANA: Even though he's lying in there it will be empty and I still need to say "it was him" "it was you" "it was him" who thrashed my life to pieces. But it wasn't him.

(Liana and Doré seem to prompt each other's words, even if reluctantly.)

DORÉ: It was never just him.
LIANA: I had the reins, in my hands. I had the. *Faith* in my capacity to *forge my life*, but then in a minute, a flash, I veered off the road. Nothing—nothing was ever really mine to do as I liked—
DORÉ: And the worst of it is—
LIANA: —the worst of it is I was sure I'd been *emptied out*, that I'd become a *hole in the wall*.

(Liana recovers herself now.)

But for quite some time now, after all that snot and sorrow, I no longer mind so much. That he left. I no longer—
DORÉ: —mind so terribly much that they took him all those years ago. I should still mind but I was dead tired of it.
LIANA: Dead tired of losing someone who was everything.
DORÉ: Only to find that even a child is not enough when that child returns.
LIANA: Only to realize that *no one* is everything, not even *him*. And the facts are that for months now—
DORÉ: —years even—

LIANA: —in the mornings when I wake, I no longer feel discarded. I no longer think of him first thing, I no longer think of. You.

DORÉ (*Agreeing*): No.

LIANA: I think instead of the *little* things, the *silly* things, like the sheer, simple delight of starting my day with the choice of slathering my toast with apple spread or thick-cut marmalade.

DORÉ: Yes. The pleasure I feel when the nuthatch comes to my window to eat the seeds I've tossed on the sill, or when I sweep the leaves from my porch, all that *crackle*.

LIANA: Yes.

(*Doré makes a move toward Liana. Liana shrinks, warning.*)

If you touch me. If you touch. Stay away. Stay the fuck away!

(*Doré hesitates. Then slowly she crouches down. At first we're not sure if Doré is collapsing or lowering herself. Then we see it's purposeful: Doré gets to her hands and knees. But it's not low enough. Doré lays down on her stomach. Liana watches her, curious and frightened. Then, slowly, very slowly, Doré begins to crawl toward Liana, intentionally, purposefully. In some wordless manner Doré is apologizing to Liana, acknowledging her pain. This crawling toward Liana is ugly, pathetic, and at moments even comical—and yet strangely moving. When Doré is close enough to touch Liana, she puts out her hand and touches Liana's hair, cheek, hesitantly, lightly. And Liana lets herself be touched. After a moment, Doré removes her hand and sits up. The two women remain seated in silence for some moments. Then Liana is suddenly cold and shivers. She buttons up her coat.*)

DORÉ: You're cold.

LIANA: So cold I'm quite sure I'll never warm up again.

DORÉ: You need a hot cup of soup. Steaming. And a lie-down. *(Beat)* I've got a spare room.

(Liana lets out a bark of laughter. Then she's quiet.)

LIANA: When can you, reasonably, be out of the flat?

DORÉ: Whenever you want me to.

(Liana thinks about this.)

LIANA: Did Dom really give you a smile?

DORÉ: Just a little one. Then she spat at my feet.

LIANA: My Dom knows how to spit.

DORÉ: I thought, "Well, she's noticed me; it's a start." *(Beat)* My flat's just up the road. A ten-minute walk.

(Liana considers some moments.)

LIANA: The facts are: I don't like crumpets. I never have . . . If you try and get into bed with me.

DORÉ: Don't be silly. You're not my type.

(Liana laughs easily for the first time.)

Do you hear that? Tiny me and tiny you. And we've just been given a good shake.

(Liana takes up her suitcase.)

LIANA: You and I were never bells.

DORÉ: Aren't we lucky then: our sounds are ugly. But we're alive.

LIANA *(Nods)*: Yes. That we are.

(Liana goes to stand in the corner now, giving Doré privacy. Doré looks at the coffin. She straightens the scarf, but leaves it where it is. Then she lightly touches the coffin with one hand.)

DORÉ: Well, my son. Good-bye. We'll see you in the trees.

(The two women move to leave the room.
    Blackout.)

END OF PLAY

GREGORY CONSTANZO

NAOMI WALLACE is a playwright from Kentucky. Her plays have been produced in the United Kingdom, Europe, the United States and the Middle East. *One Flea Spare* was incorporated in the permanent repertoire of the French national theater, the Comédie-Française. Her films include *Lawn Dogs*, *The War Boys* and *Flying Blind* (co-written with Bruce McLeod). Awards include two Susan Smith Blackburn Prizes, the Joseph Kesselring Prize, a Fellowship of Southern Writers Drama Award, an Obie Award and the Horton Foote Prize for Promising New American Play. She is also a recipient of the MacArthur "Genius" Fellowship and a National Endowment for the Arts development grant. In 2013, Wallace received the inaugural Windham-Campbell Prize for Drama, and in 2015, an American Academy of Arts and Letters Award in Literature.